Pat & Pals
Decodable Readers Theater

Words by: Sue Marasciulo
Pictures by: Mangoyu

Copyright © 2024 Sue Marasciulo.
Illustrations copyright © 2024 MangoyuArt.
All rights reserved.

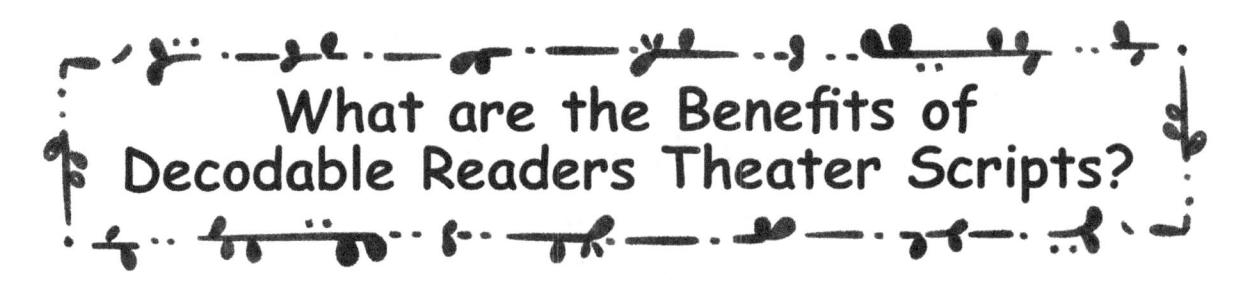

What are the Benefits of Decodable Readers Theater Scripts?

Decodable readers theater scripts are a valuable resource that combines the enjoyment of theater along with phonics practice. Let's look at the components and benefits of performing decodable readers theater scripts:

✲ Increases Motivation to Read: Readers theater scripts offer an enjoyable way to engage students and make reading more interactive and fun.

✲ Fluency Benefits: Reading and rereading helps students improve fluency - the ability to read with accuracy, speed and expression.

✲ Comprehension Benefits: reading fluency has a great impact on reading comprehension and understanding of text. Repeated readings of readers theater scripts improve fluency, allowing readers to focus more on the meaning of words than the decoding of individual words. When students expend less cognitive energy on decoding words, this frees up the cognitive load and allows room for understanding the text, resulting in deeper comprehension.

✲ Confidence Booster: Performing in front of peers helps to boost confidence in public speaking and presentation skills.

✲ Collaboration: Readers theater involves collaboration - students are required to work together to bring the script to life, thereby fostering teamwork and communication skills.

What's Included in This Book?

There are 11 readers theater scripts in this book. The scripts were developed from the first three Pat & Pals books, so children may recognize the scripts if they are familiar with **Hot Chips, Mad Fish & Other Tales, Can Ten Pigs Fit in a Tub?** and **Bed Hog & Other Tales**. There are optional character puppets included with each script that may be laminated and glued to popsicle sticks, paint stirrers, or rulers. Readers who have learned how to sound out closed syllables will be able to read most of these scripts independently. A closed syllable has a short vowel sound and ends with a consonant.

Examples: CVC (consonant-short vowel-consonant words: sad, hop, bug) and VC (short vowel-consonant words: on, it, in). Digraphs and beginning and ending blends are also included in some of these closed syllable words.

Readers Theater Tips & Suggestions

✻ Students may not be familiar with readers theater scripts and it may be helpful to model the dynamics of same.

✻ Have students highlight their characters' parts of the script.

✻ Students do not memorize their parts. Reading directly from the script is the focus of readers theater.

✻ Students must follow along with the script, even when it is not their speaking part. Students are not responsible for giving reminders when it's someone else's turn.

✻ Consider making a school copy and take-home copy of the scripts so that the students can practice at home.

✻ Consider performing for classmates, other classes, and parents! Children enjoy performing for others.

✻ Most Important Tip: HAVE FUN! If you make a mistake, it's fine...just reread the line again.

Scripts In This Book

- Pat Had A Ship
- Bud
- Zig and Zag
- The Tunnel
- Mad Bug
- The Thud
- Fluff and Stuff
- Bed Hog
- Crab Shell
- A Bug With Rot
- Red Dot Frog

NARRATOR 1	NARRATOR 2
PAT	DUCK
FOX	FROG

Pat Had a Ship

6 PARTS: NARRATOR 1, NARRATOR 2, PAT, DUCK, FOX, FROG

1. **Narrator 1:** Pat had a ship.

2. **Narrator 2:** Pat went on the ship.

3. **Narrator 1:** The ship sunk.

4. **Pat:** I am wet! I am sad! I am MAD!

5. **Pat:** A log!

6. **Narrator 2:** Pat got on the log.

7. **Frog:** I will get on the log.

8. **Duck:** I will get on the log.

9 **Fox:** I will get on the log.

10 **Narrator 1:** Pat, Frog, Duck, and Fox on a log.

11 **All:** This is fun!

12 **Narrator 2:** TIP!!!!

13 **Pat:** This is a mess!

14 **Fox:** Get on the log!

15 **Narrator 1:** Pat got on the log.

16 **Narrator 2:** Then Duck...

17 **Narrator 1:** And Fox

18 **Narrator 2:** And....

19 **Duck:** Frog?

20 **Pat:** Frog??

21 **Fox:** FROG???

22 **Duck:** Yell for Frog!

23 **Fox:** FROG!

24 **Pat:** FROG!

25 **Duck:** FROG!!

26 **Pat:** Is Frog on a rock?

27 **Frog:** Yes!

28 **Narrator 1:** Frog is on a rock!

29 **Pat:** This is not a mess!

30 **All:** This is fun!

31 **Duck:** Fun in the sun on a log!

32 **Frog:** Oh no....

33 **All:** A FIN!!!!

BUD

PAT

NARRATOR

Bud

3 PARTS: NARRATOR, PAT, BUD

1 **Narrator**: Bud is a dog.

2 **Pat**: Let's tug with a sock, Bud!

3 **Narrator**: Tug, tug, tug!

4 **Pat**: RIP!

5 **Bud**: I will run and run and run! This is fun!

6 **Pat**: No mud, Bud!

7 **Bud**: I will run in the mud! Mud is fun!

8 **Narrator**: Bud ran and ran and ran.

9   **Bud**: I will hop in the mud. I will dig in the mud. I will zig zag in the mud!

10   **Pat**: I will get your legs, Bud! I got them! Get in the bath!

11   **Narrator**: Bud got wet. Bud got a chill. Pat and Bud went in the hot sun. But...

12   **Bud**: I can run! I can run and hop back in the mud!

13   **Pat**: Oh NO!

14   **Bud**: Oh YES! Mud is fun!!!

NARRATOR

PAT

ZIG

ZAG

Zig and Zag

1. **Narrator**: Pat had a box.

2. **Pat**: I got 2 bugs in the box!

3. **Narrator**: Zig zag went the bugs!

4. **Pat**: I will call you Zig….and Zag.

5. **Zig**: Zig zag, zig zag!

6. **Zag**: Zig zag, zig, zag!

7. **Narrator**: Then the bugs got sick!

8. **Zig**: I am sick.

9. **Zag**: I am sick.

10. **Narrator**: The bugs did not zig or zag.

11. **Zig**: Tum tum bad!

12. **Zag**: Tum tum bad!

13 **Pat**: Sad bugs!

14 **Pat**: Here is a mad fish!

15 **Zig & Zag**: YUCK!

16 **Pat**: Here are hot chips!

17 **Zig & Zag**: YUCK!

18 **Pat**: Here is a fat rat!

19 **Zig & Zag**: YUCK!

20 **Zig**: Tum tum still bad!

21 **Zag**: Yes, tum tum is still bad! Help!

22 **Narrator**: Then Pat got sad. Pat let the bugs out of the box!

23 **Zig & Zag**: This is FUN!!!

24 **Narrator**: Then Pat was not sad!

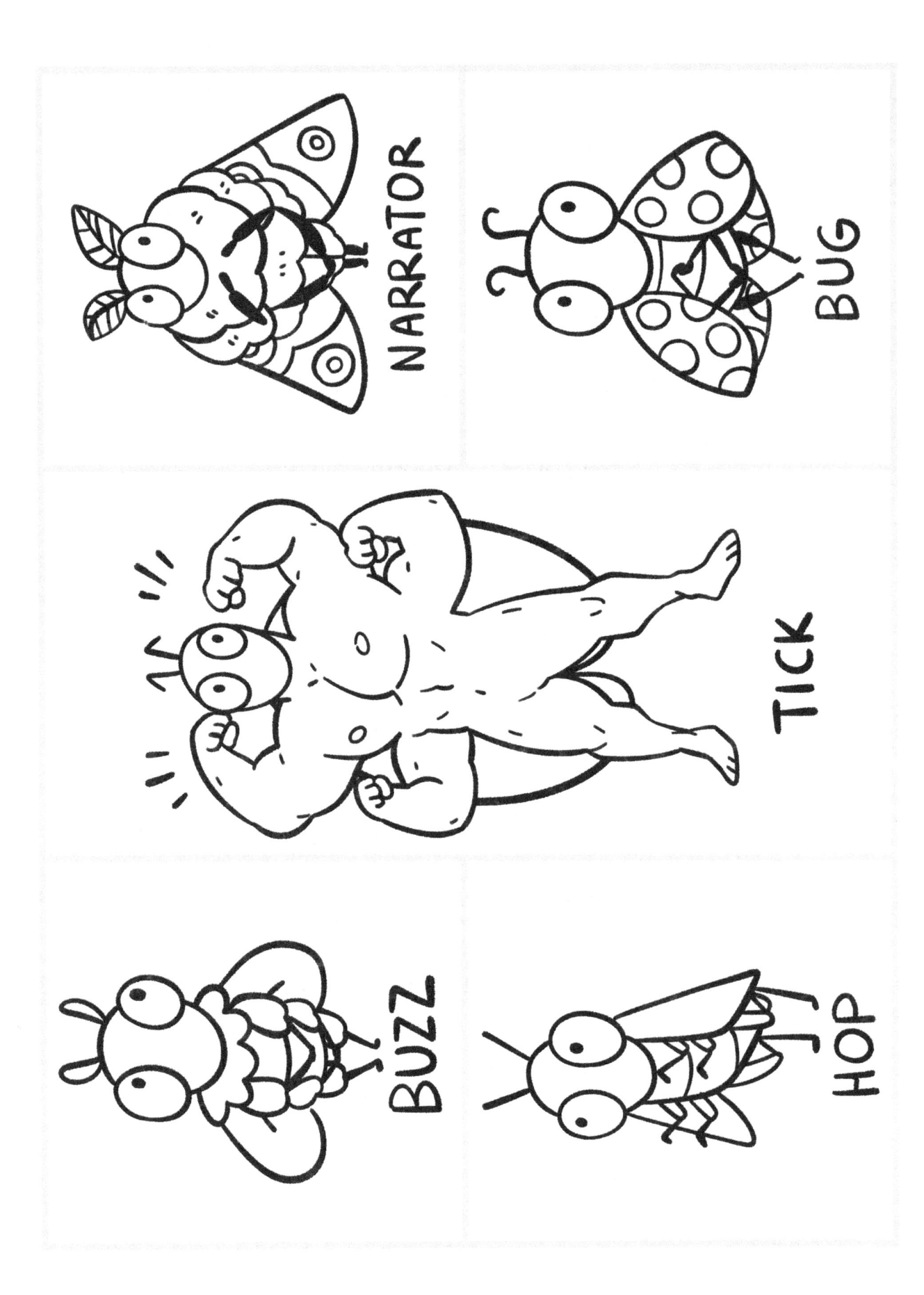

NARRATOR

BUG

TICK

BUZZ

HOP

The Tunnel

5 PARTS:

NARRATOR

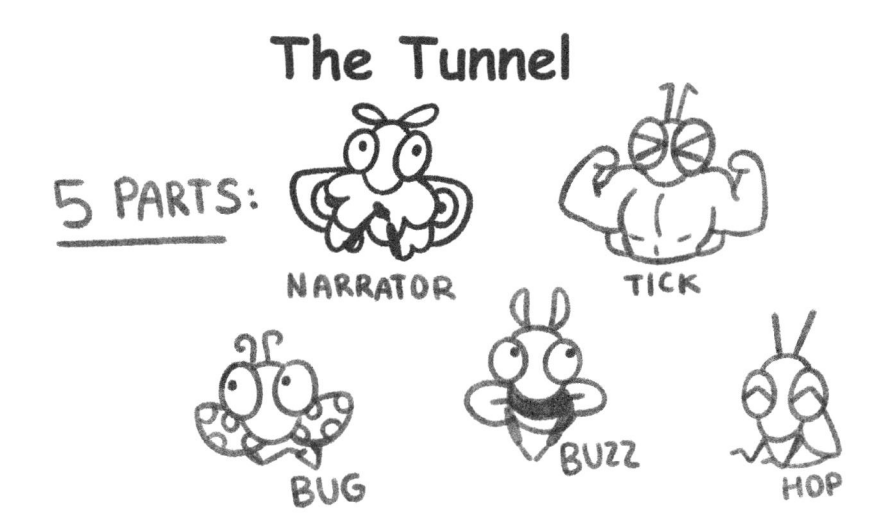

TICK

BUG

BUZZ

HOP

1   **Narrator**: Bug, Buzz, and Hop had fun!

2   **Buzz**: A big Tick! Run!!!

3   **Bug**: I will dig a tunnel!

4   **Narrator**: It was a long, long tunnel.

5   **Hop**: Quick! Get in the tunnel!

6   **Narrator**: Buzz and Hop ran into the tunnel.

7   **Tick**: I can not fit in the tunnel! Let me in! LET ME IN!

8   **Bug, Buzz & Hop**: NO! Not by the fuzz on my chinny-chin-chin! I will not let you in!

9   **Tick**: Then I will dig and dig til I fit in the tunnel!

10 **Narrator**: Bug, Buzz, and Hop ran and hid behind a rock.

11 **Tick**: I got in the tunnel. I AM NOT BAD!

12 **Buzz**: BUZZ OFF!

13 **Bug**: BUG OFF!

14 **Hop**: You are BIG!!!

15 **Narrator**: Then tick got sad.

16 **Tick**: Sob, sob, sob, sob…..and sob!

17 **Narrator**: The tunnel did fill up and they got WET!!

18 **Tick**: Quick, Hop on my back! I will get us out of the tunnel!

19 **Bug**: Tick did it!

20 **Buzz**: Thanks Tick!

21 **Hop**: Can we hug you?

22 **Tick**: Yes!

NARRATOR

PAT

BUD

MAD BUG

A Mad Bug

4 PARTS: NARRATOR   PAT   BUD   MAD BUG

1   **Bud**: A ball! A ball! I can run and get it!

2   **Pat**: Get that ball, Bud!

3   **Narrator**: Then….the ball got stuck on top of a van.

4   **Pat**: Jump Bud! Jump and get the ball!

5   **Bud**: I can not get it Pat.

6   **Narrator**: Pat got a big box and a tall stick.

7 **Pat**: I will hit the ball with the stick...WHACK!

8 **Narrator**: The ball got stuck in a web!

9 **Bud**: Yap, yap yap! I wish to get that ball back!

10 **Narrator**: The web was big and there was a Mad Bug in it!

11 **Mad Bug**: My web!!!!!!! My web got a rip!

12 **Pat**: I will fix that. I will hit the ball with a stick. WHACK!

13 **Narrator**: The ball fell in the pond.

14 **Pat & Bud**: Oh NO!

15 **Pat**: Let's run to the pond.

16 **Bud**: The ball is stuck on shells and rocks.

17 **Pat**: I will get the ball off of the shells and rocks. WHACK!

18 **Narrator**: Up, up, up and into Bud's path.

19 **Pat**: Get the ball!

20 **Narrator**: But……

21 **Mad Bug**: I got the ball and I am mad! Fix my web!

22 **Pat**: I will fix the web with jam!

23 **Narrator**: Pat and Bud made a mess with the jam. Drip, drip, drip!

24 **Mad Bug**: This is a mess. Not yet! No ball!

25 **Narrator**: Pat and Bud got rags. Pat and Bud did rub a dub dub the web!

26 **Pat**: Rub-a-dub-dub!

27 **Bud**: Rub-a-dub!

28 **Pat**: I am a mess. Lick, lick, lick! Yum! Jam!

29 **Bud**: I am a mess. Lick, lick, lick! Yum! Jam!

30 **Narrator**: Then Pat and Bud went in the pond. Rub-a-dub-dub!

31 **Pat**: Can we get the ball yet, Mad Bug?

32 **Mad Bug**: Yes!

33 **Narrator**: Bud had fun. Hop, hop, hop! Then...

34 **Bud**: Oh no! The ball went on top of the van!!!!

35 **Pat**: NO!!!!!

NARRATOR

PAT

BUD

VET

The Thud

4 PARTS:

NARRATOR

PAT

BUD

VET

1 **Bud**: Up, up, up!

2 **Narrator**: Pat and Bud ran to the top of the hill.

3 **Pat**: I am TALL!

4 **Bud**: Toss the ball! Toss the ball!! I got the ball!

5   **Pat**: Bud fell!

6   **Narrator**: Thud, thud, thud

7   **Pat**: Bud got a cut on his leg! Off to the vet!

8   **Bud**: I am sad. I can not wag.

9   **Narrator**: The vet was a man. Bud hid.

10 **Pat & Vet**: Oh no! Bud wet!

11 **Vet**: it is OK. I will get a mop and mop up that wet spot.

12 **Narrator**: Mop, mop, mop!

13 **Bud**: Can I get on your lap, Pat?

14 **Pat**: Yes!

15 **Vet**: Can I pet you?

16 **Bud**: Yes.

17 **Vet**: Let me fix that leg.

18 **Narrator**: The vet did fix Bud's leg.

19 **Bud**: Thank you! I am not sad! Kiss, kiss, kiss.

20 **Narrator**: Bud did wag and wag!

NARRATOR 1

NARRATOR 2

PAT

BUD

Fluff and Stuff

4 PARTS:

NARRATOR 1 NARRATOR 2 PAT BUD

1   **Pat**: I will be back, Bud.

2   **Narrator 1**: Pat had to go to the shop to pick up things.

3   **Bud**: I am sad.

4   **Narrator 2**: Bud got a big kiss from Pat.

5   **Pat**: kiss, kiss, kiss

6   **Bud**: I will get in my dog bed and rest.

7   **Narrator 1**: Did bud miss Pat?

8   **Bud**: Yes...

9   **Narrator 2**: He did!

10 **Bud**: Sniff, sniff, sniff. I am sad.

11 **Narrator 1**: Then Bud got a whiff of trash.

12 **Bud**: Yum, I smell trash!

13 **Narrator 2**: TIP went the trash:

14 **Bud**: Yum! Chips! Yum! Gum! Chomp, chomp, chomp!

15 **Narrator 1**: The gum got stuck on Bud's chin.

16 **Bud**: Yum! A stink of fish! Yum, yum, yum!

17 **Narrator 2**: Then Bud went back to his

dog bed.

18	**Bud**: Rip, rip, rip! Rip the bed!
19	**Narrator 1**: And the fluff fell on the rug.
20	**Bud**: Fluff is fun!
21	**Narrator 2**: Fluff got stuck on Bud's back legs.
22	**Bud**: I think that I will run and jump up!
23	**Narrator 1**: Crash went the dish!
24	**Narrator 2**: Crack went the cup!
25	**Narrator 1**: The milk did spill.
26	**Narrator 2**: The pot fell...CRASH!
27	**Bud**: This is fun!
28	**Narrator 1**: But Bud was still sad.

29 **Pat**: I miss Pat. I will run up the steps and jump on Pat's bed. Sniff, sniff, sniff... I smell Pat.

30 **Narrator 2**: Then Bud dug in Pat's bed.

31 **Narrator 1**: Bud did rip the bed.

32 **Narrator 2**: Bud did shred the bed.

33 **Narrator 1**: Fluff fell on the bed.

34 **Narrator 2**: Then....

35 **Pat**: Bud, Bud, BUD!!! A Big mess! Bud!!!

36 **Narrator 1**: Bud hid.

37 **Pat**: This is a big, big mess and I am mad!

38 **Pat**: BUD!!!!!

39 **Narrator 2**: Bud did not wag. Bud was sad.

40 **Narrator 1**: Bud got flat.

41 **Pat**: I will scrub you, Bud. I will brush you, Bud.

42 **Narrator 2**: Pat had to fix the mess and Bud had to help.

43 **Pat**: Bud, hold this dustpan.

44 **Narrator 1**: Pat and Bud swept the fluff.

45   **Pat**: I will get a mop and dunk it and get it wet.

46   **Pat**: Bud, mop up the milk. I will mop up the chips. Mop, mop, mop!

47   **Pat**: Let's pick up trash. Pick up glass and dump it in the trash.

48   **Narrator 2**: Then Bud did lick Pat's leg.

49   **Pat**: Oh, a kiss! Oh Bud! It's ok. I am not mad. Do not be sad.

50   **Narrator 1**: Hug, hug, hug. Pat and Bud did hug.

51   **Bud**: Wag, wag, wag.

BUD

PAT

NARRATOR

Bed Hog

3 PARTS: NARRATOR, PAT, BUD

1 **Narrator**: Bud was a hog in bed. His legs hit Pat in the neck!

2 **Bud**: Jab! Jab! Jab!

3 **Narrator**: Then his legs hit Pat in the back!

4 **Bud**: Kick! Kick! Kick!

5 **Pat**: Bud, do not be a big pest in bed!

6 **Narrator**: Then Bud did a big kick!

7 **Pat**: I fell off the bed and I am mad!

Bud, Bud, BUD! Get up, Bud!

8 **Bud**: I can not get up!

9 **Narrator**: Bud slept and slept and slept! Bud was such a bed hog!

10 **Pat**: I do not fit in the bed! That's it! I will get up and go in Bud's bed!

11 **Narrator**: It was small, but it was soft with lots of fluff.

Pat slept and slept and slept.

12 **Bud**: I miss Pat! I want to get snug with Pat! I will find Pat!

13 **Narrator**: Then Bud got up and went in his bed with Pat.

14   **Bud**: I will kiss Pat! Kiss, kiss, kiss!

15   **Pat**: Oh no!

16   **Bud**: Oh yes!

17   **Narrator**: And then Pat and Bud got snug in Bud's small bed!

       Pat and Bud slept and slept and slept in that small dog bed!

18   **Pat and Bud**: ZZZZZZZZZZZZZ

PAT

CRAB

NARRATOR

Crab Shell

3 PARTS

NARRATOR   CRAB   PAT

1   **Pat**: A small crab!

2   **Crab**: The shell on my back is too small! I will get rid of it!

3   **Narrator**: The crab flings the shell off of his back.

4   **Crab**: I want a big shell. I got BIG!

5   **Pat**: A red cap from a jug of milk can fit on your back!

6   **Crab**: No, no, no. This is a bad fit.

7 **Pat**: A doll's flip flop can fit on your back! It can be your shell!

8 **Narrator**: Crab fit it on his back.

9 **Crab**: No, no, no. This is a bad fit. I want a shell that will fit!

10 **Narrator**: Then Crab did zig zag zig zag in the sand.

11 **Crab**: I am sad. Sniff, sniff, sniff.

12 **Pat**: Do not get sad. I will pat you on the back.

13 **Narrator**: Then Crab got a whiff of a hot dog.

14 **Crab**: I got it! I will fit the bun on my back!

15 **Narrator**: Crab fit the bun on his back, but it fell off.

16 **Crab**: I want a shell that will fit!!!

I do not want a frog to jump on me!

I do not want a fish to get me!

I do not want a big bug to land on me!

I do not want a kid to squish me!

I am soft and I want a shell that fits!

17 **Pat**: Let's hunt for a shell that fits.

18 **Narrator**: Pat and Crab did hunt and hunt for a shell. Then Pat did trip and fell in the sand.

19 **Pat**: My hand hit a small clam shell!

20 **Narrator**: Pat held up the clam shell.

21 **Pat**: Is this it?

22 **Narrator**: Pat stuck the clam shell on Crab's back.

23 **Crab**: YES! It is the best fit! Thanks Pat!

24 **Narrator**: And Crab did a zig zag in the sand with the shell on his back.

FROG

PAT

NARRATOR

A Bug With Rot

3 PARTS:

NARRATOR

PAT

FROG

1   **Narrator**: Frog did hop on the red brick path.

2   **Frog**: The sun is hot on my back. Hop, hop, hop. This is fun! I must go to my best pal, Bud. I miss him. Hop, hop, hop.

3   **Narrator**: Then, Frog did a big hop and a flip. And Frog was on his back!

4   **Frog**: Oh no! I am stuck on the hot bricks.

5   **Narrator**: Frog did tug but his skin was stuck on the hot bricks.

6   **Frog**: This is HOT, HOT, HOT! This is bad! HELP!!!!

7   **Pat**: I think that I will go for a jog on the red brick path.

8 **Narrator**: Then Pat did stop.

9 **Pat**: A bug with rot!

10 **Frog**: Thump, thump, thump!

11 **Pat**: Oh! That is not a bug with rot! That is a frog with got stuck on hot, hot bricks! I will help you!

12 **Narrator**: Pat ran to the sink. He was fast!

13 **Pat**: I will get Frog wet!

14 **Narrator**: Drip, drip, drip. Pat got Frog wet.

15 **Pat**: Still stuck!

16   **Narrator**: Drip, drip, drip.

17   **Pat**: His legs did a kick!

18   **Narrator**: Drip, drip, drip.

19   **Pat**: Oh! Frog's chest did POP up!

20   **Narrator**: Drip, drip, drip. Then....Frog did a flip and a...

21   **Frog**: Hop, hop, hop! I will hop to the grass. I will rest and rest. I will find a path or grass or mud to get to my best pal, Bud! No hot bricks for me!

22   **Narrator**: Then Pat got a pad.

23   **Pat**: I will get a pen to tell all Frogs to get off the hot bricks!

> To all frogs:
> Get off the HOT bricks!
> It is HOT, HOT, HOT!
> You can MELT!

24   **Frog**: Thank you, Pat! Kiss, kiss, kiss!

NARRATOR

RED DOT FROG

BLACK DOT FROG

BIG DOT FROG

Red Dot Frog

4 PARTS: NARRATOR, RED DOT FROG, BLACK DOT FROG, BIG DOT FROG

1. **Narrator:** Small frogs sat in the pond. Red Dot, Black Dot, and Big Dot.

2. **Black Dot Frog:** I can hop, hop, hop.

3. **Big Dot Frog:** I can jump, jump, jump.

4 **Narrator**: But Red Dot Frog can not hop and jump. Red Dot Frog can not swim.

5 **Narrator**: All the frogs in the pond got bugs. Flick, flick, flick.

6 **Black Dot Frog**: I can get a bug for you, Red Dot Frog.

7 **Red Dot Frog**: Thanks! Yum!

8 **Big Dot Frog**: I can drag you,

Red Dot Frog.

9 **Red Dot Frog**: This is fun! But I want to get bugs too!

10 **All Frogs**: Let's think!

11 **Black Dot Frog**: Call the bugs!

12 **Red Dot Frog**: Bugs, bugs, BUGS!

13 **Narrator**: But the bugs just hid in the grass.

14 **Red Dot Frog**: No bugs! Sniff, sniff, sniff.

15 **All Frogs**: Let's think!

16 **Big Dot Frog**: Get on this raft. I can drag you to the bugs.

17 **Narrator**: Red Dot Frog got on the raft. But the bugs left in a rush. Red Dot Frog wept.

18 **Red Dot Frog**: Sniff, sniff, sniff. I want to get bugs!

29 **All Frogs**: Let's think!

20 **Red Dot Frog**: A stick, a stick! A stick can help! I can grip the stick!

21 **Black Dot Frog**: Dip the stick in sap!

22 **Red Dot Frog**: Yes!! The bugs will stick to the sap.

23 **Narrator**: Then Red Dot Frog

held the stick...and a bug did land on the stick!

24 **Red Dot Frog**: SNAP! MUNCH, MUNCH, MUNCH! Yum! I did it! I got a bug!

25 **Narrator**: Then....all the frogs in the pond did a chant...

26 **All Frogs**: HE DID IT! HE DID IT!

27 **Red Dot Frog**: This is fun! I will get bugs for all my pals in the pond!

28 **Narrator**: And he did!

Author Bios

Sue Marasciulo is a retired elementary Special Education teacher. Her passion is helping children with dyslexia to feel more confident in their abilities and gifts. Throughout her many years of teaching, she was inspired by her students' fortitude, adaptability to learn, and ability to excel in many areas.

Sue lives in South Carolina with her husband, Al, and their two rescued dogs, Scrappy Doo and Sunny. Sue has three sons, Matt, Greg, and JP. Greg is a professional wrestler with AEW and every now and again, Sue makes a brief appearance on the show with her famous van!

For more information visit suemarasciulo.com

Mangoyu, also affectionately known as Mango, spent the 2020 pandemic online happily bothering wrestlers with funny cartoon drawings of themselves, blissfully unaware that someday, the beloved world-famous Sue (mother of wrestler Trent Beretta) would discover her silly wrestling doodles. Two years later, Sue would ask Mango to join her on the exciting adventure of illustrating a children's books for kids with dyslexia.

The duo are still going strong and are gleefully scheming to add many more stories and books to their Pat & Pals collection.

Made in the USA
Las Vegas, NV
31 May 2024